Devotions
for teens on
family survival

DOES ANYBODY UNDERSTAND?

KAREN
DOCKREY

C H A R I O T
FAMILY PUBLISHING

In memory of my grandfather,
Fred C. Smith, who believed in me and demonstrated
family love for and to me.
He accepted me without condition, listened to me and
talked with me, understood my fears and dreams, and
encouraged me to become the best I could be.

Chariot Family Publishing™ is a division of David C. Cook Publishing Co.
David C. Cook Publishing Co., Elgin, Illinois 60120
David C. Cook Publishing Co., Weston, Ontario
Nova Distribution, Ltd., Newton Abbot, England

DOES ANYBODY UNDERSTAND? DEVOTIONS FOR TEENS ON FAMILY SURVIVAL
© 1992 by Karen Dockrey

Portions of this book were previously published as articles in *event!* (April 1987;
August 1987; September 1987; December 1987; June 1988), a leisure reading
periodical for youth. © Copyright The Sunday School Board of the Southern
Baptist Convention. All rights reserved. Used by permission.

Cover photo by Dave DeJong
Photo colorizing by Gary Gnidovic
Cover design by Rick Schroeppel
First printing, 1992
Printed in the United States of America

96 95 94 93 92   1 2 3 4 5

TABLE OF CONTENTS

Communication

1
They Don't Understand!

My mom never listens to me. Whenever I talk about school she interrupts, lectures, and closes the subject. How can she give all that advice without even hearing my problem?

The only thing my parents and I have in common is living in the same house. I'm always mad at them or they're mad at me.

Poor communication lurks behind many parent problems. When people misunderstand each other, they become defensive, lash out, and remain frustrated. Some refuse to talk at all, keeping their anger and pain inside.

But here's good news: communication is a skill, and like any skill it can be learned. With God's help, you can develop healthy, effective, loving communication.

The most important areas are usually the ones that are hardest to discuss. Circle three areas you and your parents have trouble talking about.

grades	curfew	church
friends	money	chores
dating	music	sex

Check God's Word

Read Romans 12:9-21. What actions described here could strengthen communication in your household?

Talk It Over with God

Use these sentence starters to begin a conversation with God about communication:

- God, my family finds it easy to talk when . . .
- God, my family finds it hard to talk when . . .
- An action from Romans 12 that might make the hard times easier is . . .
- God, I know You want me to . . . , but I have trouble doing it. Help me . . .

Apply It to You

Choose the phrase from Romans 12:9-21 that applies most specifically to your family's communication problems. Write it in your own words with your name and problem inserted. Example:

"When my dad refuses to listen to me, I will *overcome evil with good* by listening to him. That might encourage him to listen to me next time."

Believe it or not, your parents are simply teenagers who have grown a little older. How can seeing them as people who share your dreams and fears make it easier to communicate with them?

2
Why Don't They Say What They Mean?

Mom fears her daughter will get hurt by dating a certain boy. She thinks, *If I keep you away from that boy, I can keep you from hurting.* So she says, "You can't go out with him anymore." Mom wants her daughter to be happy. She thinks, *If I tell you how to find happiness, you won't have to struggle for it.* So she says, "That boy won't make you happy. Date this one."

The lack of logic in Mom's thinking is obvious, but logic doesn't keep her from feeling and thinking certain things. She knows with her head that her daughter must make her own choice—but her heart wants to protect her.

The same is true for the daughter, who knows with her head that God wants her happy and that the boyfriend in question makes her more miserable than happy. But when her mom starts in, the daughter wants to say, "I might decide to break up with him, but I want it to be my choice. When you tell me he's not good enough for me, I want to stay with him just to prove you wrong!"

Why can't the two of them just say what they really mean or feel? Because it's hard to be honest. Most people fear that if they're honest, someone will take advantage of them.

Check God's Word
As you observe your parents and siblings, notice ways you avoid saying what you really mean and feel. Then make your words communicate what you want to say. Ephesians 4:29-32 suggests guidelines for doing this. Write down some actions from these verses that could improve communication at your house.

Notice "building others up" in verse 29. This means making it easier for others to live the Christian life. When you tell your parents your thoughts, feelings, and fears, you make it easier for both you and them to follow Jesus. The same thing happens when you listen to their thoughts, feelings, and fears.

Talk It Over with God
Talk with God about communicating clearly.
- God, what could my parents do to make it easier for me to talk honestly? Positively? How could I make it easier for them?
- God, what I really want to say to my parents is . . .
- God, what I really want them to say to me is . . .

Apply It to You
Wouldn't it be great if we could just tell each other our fears, hopes, dreams, and ideas, and talk about

9

them in an atmosphere of acceptance? It won't be easy, but work toward this ideal with your parents. Translate your feelings and thoughts into words that grow closeness, not chaos. Fill in the first two columns and then in the third write words that follow Ephesians 4:29. Notice the sample:

WHEN I	I THINK	SO I WILL SAY
Fear my mom is trying to tell me what to do.	She doesn't trust me.	"Will you give me ideas rather than orders? I want to make my own choice."

3

It's Impossible to Talk to My Parents

My friends understand my feelings, but my
parents tell me how to feel. My aunt listens,
but my parents lecture. My teacher helps me
think through my ideas, but my parents panic
when they hear something they don't like.
What makes talking to parents harder than
talking to anyone else?

Close contact. Because you live with your parents,
you show them more of your bad side and they
show you more of theirs. You take your problems
out on each other.

Desire for independence. You want to make your
own decisions, and rightly so. But your parents may
hear your requests for independence as rejection.
You may hear their help as control.

Need for love. Your parents frustrate you precisely
because you want their approval and
understanding. Because they are important to you,
their criticism and accusations hurt.

11

Differing tastes. What appeals to you in music, clothes, language, and hairstyle may repel your parents and vice versa. Some differences are pesky but harmless. Other times you or your parents have a genuine gripe.

Authority. Because your parents have the power to enforce their word, you may find it hard to talk honestly and openly. Parents control money, the car keys, and many other privileges.

History. Your parents may have suffered because of a poor choice. If they see you heading toward that same choice, they may panic or tighten their grip.

Hectic schedules. Jobs, school, time with friends, meetings, church activities, sports, and other commitments keep each family member running. For some families it is rare to be in the house at the same time and even rarer to spend time together.

Check God's Word
Because Jesus grew up on earth as a real kid with real parents, He understands both the pleasures and the difficulties of talking with parents. Luke 2:41-52 records a time when Jesus' parents did not understand Him.

How did Jesus talk with His parents even during a misunderstanding? Notice the path from parental worry (v. 48) to discussion (v. 49) to Jesus' obedience (v. 51) to growth (v. 52).

Jesus could have flown off the handle when His mother said she worried. After all, He hadn't done anything wrong. Instead He calmly explained where He had been and why.

Talk It Over with God

Jesus was both fully human and fully divine. That means He experienced every human emotion and lived them exactly the way God wants humans to live (Hebrews 2:17, 18). Because He's been through what you go through, He is a great source of advice for communication barriers.

Talk with Jesus about a talking difficulty you and your parents currently face.

- Jesus, my parents and I go different directions when . . .
- I've tried talking, but that doesn't seem to work. What else could I try?

Apply It to You

Identify two of your family's communication obstacles. Now choose one and circle the reason you think the obstacle occurs (from the paragraphs found at the beginning of this lesson).

Finally, write an action or attitude you could express to make it easier to talk.

4
Nothing Works

All these ideas sound great, but they just won't work with my family. My mom insists on telling me what to do, and if I ask to talk about it she says I'm disrespectful. I've tried listening and talking calmly. My mom just says that she's the mother.

Peace and communication at home have a frustrating catch: both parent and teen have to work together. If a parent is not willing or able to work toward communication, it won't happen.

But there's a fortunate "catch to this catch": the peace-building actions of one family member can encourage another to cooperate. Because you can't change the actions or attitudes of your parents, begin by changing your own. It's not easy, but it can work.

Check God's Word
Notice ideas in Romans 12:18 and 14:19 for communicating when it seems impossible.

- "If it is possible." Peace is not "possible" if you, your parent, or your sibling isn't working for it.
- "As far as it depends on you." Do your best with your own actions and attitudes. Your positive outlook and peace-building actions just might encourage your mom or dad to work for peace and clear communication.
- "Pursue." Peaceful communication is a process, not an instant miracle. Be willing to keep on keeping on, even when your efforts don't immediately pay off.
- "Building up of one another." When you know someone likes you, you feel secure with her. You relax and tell her your thoughts, dreams, and ideas. She listens to and understands you. You can help create this mutual security in your family by genuinely building up family members.

Which of the above four phrases do you need most in your family? Circle it. Ponder how you'll do it.

Talk It Over with God
Sometimes it's hard to understand just how God's advice works. Talk with Him about the two verses you just read.

- God, it doesn't seem possible for clear communication in my house when . . .
- God, I'm quick to blame my parent or sibling for communication problems. One action or attitude that depends on me is . . .
- God, I could build up my family by . . .

15

Apply It to You

With your closest friends you tend to compensate for the bad and concentrate on the good. Try the same with your family.

- Tell your parent/sibling when they do something right ("Thanks for listening, Dad"). People tend to repeat what you compliment.
- Tell them when you're hurt so they'll know what to avoid.
- Every time they do something that bugs you, think of two things they do well.

5

Lemme Out of Here!

My parents try to control what I do, where I go, who I spend time with, and how I spend my money. I can hardly wait until I get out on my own. Then I can do things the way I want to do them!

Communicating with your parents is more than a survival tool till independence. When you get out on your own, you'll need communication skills for getting along with everyone you come in contact with. Good communication skills make difficult relationships tolerable and happy relationships happier.

Check God's Word
It's especially hard to communicate with parents when they act unfairly. But look at Jesus. Listeners rejected His teachings as lies. His closest friends misunderstood His identity and purpose. He was crucified for claiming to be God when He really was God.

Jesus deserved better treatment. Yet rather than

pouting about it, He let God equip Him to keep the kind of attitude that makes closeness and understanding possible.

Read Philippians 2:1-18.

Some people who read these verses think God wants us to be doormats, but they're missing the true meaning of humility. True humility is summarized in verse 4. It considers the interests of other family members as important as one's own. This results in cooperation, sensitivity, listening, and understanding.

Obviously the best humility is mutual. "Doormatism" can be as dangerous as total selfishness. (For example, the child or spouse of an alcoholic who hides the problem allows the drinking and pain cycle to continue.) True family humility breaks the pain cycle to bring joy. Humility sees all needs as important and works to produce God's kind of love in the family.

Talk It Over with God
Jesus not only modeled the attitude to take during conflict, He offers the strength to do it. Read Philippians 4:13.
- Jesus, it's not fair when . . . To respond with Your attitude I could . . .
- Jesus, imitating Your attitude doesn't mean to be silent. One way to show love is to express needs. I need to tell . . . that I need . . . by . . .
- Another way to show love is to talk out anger, rather than shout or keep it in. I could say . . .

Apply It to You
Memorize Philippians 4:13 by substituting a

different communication barrier each time you
repeat it. For example:
- "I can share my feelings and needs honestly
  through Christ who gives me strength."
- "I can listen without judgment through Christ
  who gives me strength."
- "I can communicate my love for my parents
  through Christ who gives me strength."

What communication patterns do your parents
have that you want to imitate? What communication
patterns do they use that you don't want to repeat?
Substitute a positive communication pattern for each.

Trust

1
Why Won't They Give Me a Chance?

Everybody gets to stay out until midnight but me. My parents say I can stay out later as I get older, but I don't think it has to do with age at all. They just don't trust me.

Trust is more than something you have or don't have. It's a daily give-and-take of information, a process of communication, a sharing of dreams and ideas, a willingness to negotiate needs. Problems come when you want to demonstrate your responsible behavior in a given situation and your parents won't allow you the opportunity.

Check God's Word
It's good that you want to prove yourself. God, like your parents, is interested in how well you handle responsibility.

Read Luke 16:10-12. Jot down some ways you have been "trustworthy with little." Jot down some ways you have been "dishonest (untrustworthy) with little."

What other actions and attitudes might help

you prove your trustworthiness or overcome your previous dishonesty?

Talk It Over with God

Talk with God about earning your parents' trust. Use these sentence starters as guides.

- God, my parents never let me . . .
- I know I'm not quite ready for . . . , but I think I am ready for . . .
- I might be able to get them to let me . . . if . . .
- God, help me prove I can be trusted to . . . by . . .

Apply It to You

Jot down all the things you want your parents to let you do. Next to each, write something like it that they already let you do. Plan a way to move from what you have to what you want. Then talk over your ideas with your mom and dad.

For example:

I WANT	I HAVE
to have friends over when my parents are not home.	the privilege of having friends over when my parents are home.

MY PLAN
I can ask my mom to observe my friends and me when she is around and then ask her to choose one she thinks I'd be "safe" with. She could call to check on us.

Trust is hard to build because parents are afraid you'll get hurt or hurt someone. Why do you think they lecture or nag rather than share their fears?

2
Destroying Trust

While it takes a long time to earn your parents' trust, it can be destroyed in an instant. Here are five reliable ways to destroy your parents' trust in you.

Never answer questions. Nothing drives parents crazier than answers like "I don't know" or "I can't remember."

Never volunteer information. Especially when you're good, don't tell your parents about it. If they have no evidence you can be trusted, they'll believe you're always up to something.

Get defensive. If you slip and answer a question, be certain to act defensive about it. Look as suspicious as you can so your parents will think you're lying.

Accuse them of mistrust. If your parents continue to ask who you went with, where you went, and what you did, say to them: "You don't trust me or you wouldn't ask all these questions!"

Refuse to learn from mistakes. When you blow it, cover it up rather than face it.

Check God's Word
Obviously, the way to build trust is to do the opposite of the five suggestions above. All are based

on talking. Talk with your parents to show you can be trusted, to smooth over past instances of broken trust, to work out disagreements on areas of trust.

Underline tips for talking from Ephesians 4:25-27 and I Timothy 4:7. Write in your own words what you underlined. Then compare your tips to these.

- Remove any hint of lying or truth stretching (v. 25)
- Talk calmly about anger rather than hurting your parent with it (v. 26).
- Notice and deny myths like "parents just want to spoil your fun" (v. 7).
- Recognize that learning to talk honestly with parents is a process just like training for a sport. It's hard but worth it (v. 7).

Talk It Over with God
Talk with God about building trust through talking with your parents.

- God, I destroy trust in my home when . . .
- It's especially hard to talk to my parents about trust when they interrupt or lecture or . . . The talking tip that would help us the most is . . .
- To gain my parents' trust . . .

Apply It to You
Check off actions you are willing to do to build, rather than destroy, trust:

- Tell my parents at least two things I do or feel daily, so they won't have to ask.
- Answer questions calmly and without defensiveness.

25

- Remind myself that parents ask questions because they care.
- Admit it when I make a mistake that breaks trust, ask for forgiveness, and work out a plan to build back trust.

3

I've Already Blown It

Even the best of the best blow it. The disciple Peter, a dedicated follower of Jesus, fiercely declared his loyalty to Jesus and then betrayed Jesus the same day. As you study these passages, think about a time when you betrayed someone's trust.

Check God's Word
Read about Peter's promise of faithfulness and betrayal in Luke 22:31-34, 54-62.

After Peter betrayed Jesus, Jesus not only took Peter back, but gave him an important responsibility. Read John 21:15-19.

Jesus saw the potential in Peter even after Peter had failed. This is not easy for very human and vulnerable parents to do–nor is it easy for you to trust your parents after they have betrayed you. What elements in the second passage might help you earn back trust after you've blown it? Notice:
- Jesus expected Peter to do well after blowing it and to learn from his failure.
- Peter listened even though he was hurt that Jesus asked the same question repeatedly.
- Peter got a bit defensive, but kept calm.
- Peter accepted Jesus' challenge to do the right

thing from then on. (Read about Peter in the book of Acts. He became one of the strongest leaders in the church. He stood up firmly for Jesus under the worst of pressures.)

• Jesus asked Peter if he loved Him, indicating that love is the basis for serving Jesus and for building trust.

When trust gets rocky, remember how much you love, or want to love your parents. Then show that love through trust-building actions.

Talk It Over with God

Gaining trust back is seldom easy or quick, but is worth the work. Talk with God about it.

• My parents may find it hard to trust me because . . .
• They probably fear that I'll . . .
• My parents and I can work together to be sure I don't make another wrong choice by . . .
• God, help me to depend more on Your Holy Spirit's power to . . .

Apply It to You

Practice in your head a conversation between you and your parents about gaining trust back. Include details about the betrayal of trust and why you think it happened. Ask forgiveness and discuss actions that will re-earn trust. Anticipate several different reactions your parents might have and what you would say to each.

Now, take courage . . . and go have that conversation.

Remember, one reason parents have trouble trusting is that they want to spare you their mistakes. They don't want you to hurt like they have.

When both of you are in a good mood, ask your parents to tell you about a time they suffered because of a poor choice. Ask: What would you like me to learn from your experience?

4
"I Wish They'd Let Me . . ."

I wish my parents would let me stay out later.

I wish my parents would let me keep my room the way I want it.

I wish my parents would trust me to choose my own friends!

What might these teenagers do and say to negotiate their parents' trust? Look for answers in the following Bible verses.

Check God's Word
Find tips for negotiating trust in these verses:
Proverbs 15:1; 22:11; 1:8; 3:6.
   Did you find these negotiation tips?
   • Use a caring, not critical tone. Attitude is as important as what you say.
   • Be honest. A "pure heart" won't deceive just to get what it wants.
   • Parents respond to genuine and caring words

that don't "butter up." These can be called gracious words.

- Be willing to learn. When you allow, even encourage, your parents' advice in the area you want trust, they more likely grant the trust.
- Act in ways that please God. If you're pleasing God, your goals will be good ones and your parents will likely agree with them.

Talk It Over with God

Talk with God about the trust and privileges you want to negotiate.

- God, I wish my parents would let me . . .
- The proverbs I've just read explain that the best things for me to do about this wish are . . .
- God, I admit I have an attitude problem about . . .
- God, help me be open to advice about . . .

Apply It to You

Agree with your parents to make "wish lists." Write what you want from each other, avoiding being critical or harsh. When the lists are complete, take turns requesting one wish from your list. Commit to grant each other at least three wishes. Example:

MOM	TEEN
1. Pick up your room.	1. Give me a decent curfew.
2. Call if you'll be late.	2. Stop the silent treatment.
3. Tell me about what you do.	3. Trust me.

31

4. Understand that I
   care.
5. Talk to me about
   problems.

4. Let me have
   privacy.
5. Show me you care.

Trust earning is gradual. Trust granting is also mutual; you grant trust to your parents as they grant it to you. Recall wishes your parents have made in the past. How might you grant them now?

5

Sibling Wars

Did you wear my blouse again? I planned to wear it today and I found it in the laundry! Why can't you ask first?

You said you wouldn't tell. Now you've spilled it to everyone at school. Why can't you consider my feelings before you blab my secrets?

Sisters and brothers, stepsisters and stepbrothers, add a whole new dimension to family trust. Most people are more concerned about others taking care of their things and their secrets than they are about caring for other people and their things.

The obvious solution is to care for others the way we want to be cared for. Though simple to say, it's hard to do. Deliberately change your self-focus into other-focus. As *you* change, you'll earn the privilege of requesting change in your siblings.

Check God's Word
Building trust between yourself and your siblings begins by obeying God. Notice the delightful promises in Psalm 37:3-9.

33

God cares about you and your needs. These needs include a trusting relationship between you and your sister(s) or brother(s). Notice that obeying God's guidelines opens the way for Him to give you the good things you need and want. What good actions might God suggest for solving the conflicts you and your siblings face?

Talk It Over with God
The best trust between siblings is mutual. Let these sentence starters guide your talk with God about the trust between you and your sibling.
- God, I really get upset when [sibling] . . .
- A "trust in the Lord and do good" action that could help this problem is . . .
- I probably drive [sibling] crazy when I . . .
- To keep from doing this I could . . .

How would earning your sister or brother's trust increase the chance that she or he might work to earn yours?

Apply It to You
Using every letter of the alphabet, name twenty-six ways to "trust in the Lord and do good" that could build trust between you and your siblings. Each time you get stuck, reread Psalm 37:3-9.
Examples:
- Ask sister to check before wearing my clothes.
- Be an example by asking before I wear her clothes.
- Clear the air by talking calmly when I'm angry.
- Determine not to break confidences.
- Erase demands and substitute requests.

Understanding

1

I Don't Even Understand Myself!

I'm so confused. Sometimes I can think clearly and act in ways I'm proud of. Other times I get all crazy or emotional, and I embarrass myself. I know hormones are responsible for some of this, but I'm not sure how or why. One minute I want my parents to cuddle me, and the next minute I get mad if they try. I want them to bear with me, to help me understand my changing self, to help me become the person I want to be.

The years between childhood and adulthood are both delightful and frustrating. While you can be proud that you've outgrown much of your childishness, the transition probably isn't happening as quickly as you want it to. One minute you feel and act like an adult, and the next like a child. You sometimes have trouble understanding yourself, let alone asking someone else to understand you.

Even adults fight the maturity battle. They're still growing toward being the people God wants them to be. They're still trying to understand themselves and what God wants them to do. Find encouragement in the midst of your confusion by keeping your eyes on God's goals for you.

Check God's Word
God is your guide for understanding yourself. Read I Corinthians 13:8-13.

Paul, who wrote this passage, was still becoming the man God wanted him to be. He could see some progress ("Now I know in part") but had not arrived ("then I shall know fully").

As you let God and other people know you, you begin to understand yourself better. Letting God know you helps you become the happiest, most understanding, and most complete person you can be.

Talk It Over with God
What do you want to understand about yourself? What sort of person are you becoming? What actions and attitudes will bring the happiness you seek? Talk with God about it:
- God, one thing I want to know fully is . . .
- Being caught between childhood and adulthood is frustrating when . . .
- Knowing You understand makes me feel . . .

Apply It to You
Write a letter to your parents telling them what you think about and how you feel. Help them

understand what kind of person you want to be and why. Share with them some of the confusion you experience. Let them know you're interested in God's plan for you. Invite their interest, prayer, and encouragement.

Reread the letter and edit out any negativism, criticism, or defensiveness. Make it a letter that draws you closer, rather than vents everything you've been mad about for the last year.

2

What Parents Wish Their Teens Knew about Parents

I feel bad when I take my frustrations out on you. Because I can't yell at my boss, I end up exploding at home. It's not fair to you and I'm sorry. Please forgive me.

I find it unbelievably hard to be a parent, especially when we're having problems. Please understand I want to keep talking even when things get tense.

I want you to be happy. I want you to have good friends. I want you to feel smart, likable, and competent. I want you to feel free to talk with me about your worries, joys, problems. Even more than talking to me, I want you to turn to God for answers. Please know that even when I don't say it, I love you.

Can you imagine your parents saying any of those things? What else do you think your parents want you to understand about them?

Check God's Word
What happens to understanding when you and your parents go through tense times? Rather than letting problems divide, let them motivate you to work toward clearer understanding. Underline phrases in Galatians 6:2-5 that might help you do this.

How can you and your parents help each other with problems when you're so different? Your specific experiences haven't been the same, but your feelings have: You've both felt pain. You've both yearned for understanding. You've both needed patience when you're in a bad mood. You've both wanted support to make good decisions and follow them up.

Let your similar feelings motivate you to understand and care for each other even when the specifics are very different.

You and your parents can become a team. Certainly this is a dream, but it's a dream you can help make come true. Work toward sharing your burdens with your parents as they share theirs with you.

Talk It Over with God
How can you bear each other's burdens and so fulfill the law of Christ in your family?
- God, a burden, problem, or rough circumstance that currently threatens understanding in my family is . . .

- The problem makes me act strange by . . .
- It makes my parents act strange by . . .
- I think You want me to help bear this burden by . . .

Apply It to You
When one family member does all the burden bearing, that person gets used, taken advantage of, or ignored. Who in your family most needs your help and understanding right now?

Invite each of your parents to write you a letter telling what they want you to know about how they think, feel, and act. Explain that just as you want them to understand you, you want to understand them.

3
Times Have Changed

There wasn't as much pressure to drink or do drugs when my parents were teenagers.

They get all bent out of shape when I see an R-rated movie. I'm not going to go out and have sex just because I see a movie about it.

Have things changed since your parents were teenagers? Yes and no. Yes, the pressure to drink and take drugs is greater, because it's more socially acceptable. Yes, movies are more revealing and abusive than they used to be.

But no, life hasn't changed in the basic ways. Destructive drugs have been around for generations. Out-of-marriage sex has always been a serious temptation with lifelong consequences.

Check God's Word
After reading each of these verses in your Bible, jot a truth about dealing with today's problems and temptations: Proverbs 20:1; Psalm 86:14-15;

Proverbs 10:6; Proverbs 5:18-20; Proverbs 5:21-22;
I Corinthians 10:13.

Let God equip you to resist temptation. Make
resisting easier by recognizing that the wrong itself
will bring consequences even if you don't "get
caught." Make it easier by staying away from
tempting circumstances and requesting supervision.

Talk It Over with God
Pain is pain. Whether it's worse now than when
your parents grew up or not, your pain still hurts
you. Talk with God about it.
- God, I know drinking is wrong, but those who
  drink seem to have more fun . . .
- Lord, when I see the results of drinking and
  drug use . . .
- God, sex in movies and songs . . .
- I know You can equip me to make choices that
  will bring happiness. One I face now is . . .

Apply It to You
Ask your parents what life was like when they were
teenagers.
- What temptations did you face? How did you
  resist them?
- What did your parents say and do about the TV
  and movies that you watched?
- How do you see life as the same as when you
  were a teenager? How is it different?
  Do your parents seem to have forgotten what
being a teenager is like? If they haven't forgotten,
what makes their memories so vivid?

4

Brother and Sister Complications

If I even think about doing anything wrong, my sister tells on me. My parents always believe her and never believe me.

Most of the time my sister and I get along great. We can talk about everything. She's like a best friend.

How can siblings be so lovable and hate-able at the same time? One of these factors is usually responsible:

- You live closely and show both your best and worst sides.
- You compete for the same parents' attention.
- Age, interests, and skills can make you compatible or incompatible.
- You live with the same parents and deal with similar personalities and circumstances. This makes it easy for you and your sibling to understand each other.

Check God's Word
Because it's easier to notice sibling pain, we'll study a passage that explains how to respond to a sibling who has hurt you. These verses refer to brothers and sisters in Christ, but the principles work with family brothers and sisters as well.

Read Matthew 18:15-20 and write the verse that describes each step.

___ Explain privately what s/he did wrong and how it hurt you. (Notice that you go to him/her rather than waiting for an apology.)

___ If s/he listens to you, rejoice about being close again.

___ If s/he doesn't listen, ask for help, perhaps from your parent or parents.

___ Take the problem to the whole family (your at-home "church").

___ If s/he still won't listen, keep trying to win him/her over with kindness

___ Keep trying to get along, realizing that together you can do more than either of you can do alone (3 verses).

Talk It Over with God
See your sister(s) and brother(s) as fellow believers or potential fellow believers. Talk with God about this.

- God, I'm crazy about my sister/brother when . . .
- God, my sister/brother drives me crazy when . . .
- Knowing You love both of us and want our happiness makes me . . .

Apply It to You
Try one more letter, realizing that letters can communicate the things you might be embarrassed

to say aloud. Write a letter to one of your brothers or sisters, saying why you like that person and what you hope for him or her

Let this letter break down a barrier, create a bond, or erase a frustration. Pray that God will use the letter His way.

5

Why Can't We Be Happy like Everyone Else?

All these tips for understanding will work if you have the right kind of family. My family is not the happy, loving type. We disagree and argue, rather than get along. If we really loved each other, wouldn't we have less trouble communicating and understanding each other?

No family is problem free. The best families are those who learn how to resolve their differences, not those who have none. Understanding never comes automatically, but must be learned and developed.

The first step toward creating family understanding is commitment. Each family member must decide to love the others enough to understand them.

Your making this decision can encourage the rest of your family to do so. Commit yourself to express love for your parents and siblings even when you don't like them. Commit to understand and encourage them the way God understands and encourages you. Commit to talk through problems rather than let them consume you.

Check God's Word
Did you know that deciding to understand your parents and siblings can be a way to worship God? Read Romans 12:1-5.

When you offer yourself to God, He will guide you to understand your family and give you the right words to invite your parents to understand you. The closeness that grows from this kind of understanding pleases God. Because it pleases God, it is a type of worship. Because pleasing God ultimately pleases you, offering yourself to God brings happiness.

Verse 2 explains that the world's plan for happiness doesn't work very well. God offers alternatives: lasting marriage, recognizing and meeting the needs of children, closeness, and answers to anger.

Talk It Over with God
Talk with God about building understanding in your family.
- One pattern of the world that messes up understanding in my family is . . .
- One attitude You need to transform in me is . . .
- God, thanks for wanting to work in me to help create family happiness. I commit myself to . . .

Apply It to You

Watch an episode of a TV show about a family.
Which of their actions destroy understanding?
Which actions build understanding? Which of the
following "patterns of the world" do you see in the
TV family?

Match each pattern in the left-hand column
below to a "transformed-by-God" pattern that will
truly create happiness.

PATTERNS OF WORLD

- Just leave when home gets unbearable.
- Look out for your own interests.
- Expect parents to give you whatever you want.
- Sneak around if your parents ground you.
- Let the most forceful win.
- Be sarcastic rather than direct.

TRANSFORMED PATTERNS

- So everyone can win, work together, considering each member's interests.
- Talk over unfair rules; ask to earn privileges.
- Find help when family problems get unbearable.
- Expect to give as well as get from your parents.
- When mad, say so directly, rather than hint with sarcasm.
- Swallow your pride.

Conflict

1
They Don't Like Me

All of a sudden my parents have become my
enemies. They want me to come in early.
They insist on dictating what I do and think.
They criticize my friends. Why can't we get
along anymore?

Now that you're an adolescent, you require a
deeper level of understanding, more precise
communication, and a more mutual relationship.
These changes don't always come easily.

As a child you requested affection by snuggling
in your daddy's lap. Now you want affection that
includes approval and reassurance. You notice this
in areas like these:

- As a child you obeyed your parents to please
  them. You still want to please them, but you
  want pleasing to go beyond obedience. You want
  your parents to understand and approve of your
  ideas, your decisions, your dreams, your feelings.
- As a child you wanted to spend all your time
  with your parents. Your love for them is still
  strong, but you want more time with friends.

Your parents' struggles are similar.

- It's easy to cuddle a child on your lap and tease her. It's harder to show affection for a teen who still needs your physical love, but may be embarrassed by your hug.
- It's easy to tell a child what to do and expect instant obedience. It's harder to negotiate face-to-face with a teen whose ideas are often as good as yours.
- It's easy to make up games for a child's party. It's harder to agree on fun with a teen who is part child/part adult.

Rather than signaling the end of closeness with your parents, these new relationship dynamics indicate the need for a more mature type of closeness, a closeness that can be even stronger than before.

Check God's Word

The apostle James was a firm believer in Christianity that made a difference in everyday life. His suggestions in James 4:1-3, 7, 8, 11a can help create family closeness in the midst of conflict.

What desires battle within you? Wanting to make your own decisions? Struggling to communicate your ideas? Recognizing the person you are and deciding what you like and what you want to change?

Instead of quarreling with your parents over these issues, work on them together. Ask God to help your family turn conflict into closeness.

Talk It Over with God
Talk with God about how to use your growing
maturity as an asset, not a hindrance, to family
closeness.
- A battle within me that causes fights and
  quarrels with my parents is . . .
- I tend to slander (cut down, say hurtful words)
  most when . . .
- Help me substitute words that build closeness
  instead, such as . . .

Apply It to You
List ways you are more mature now than you were
as a child. Why does greater maturity bring both
pleasure and pain? How is the pleasure worth the
pain?

2

They Don't Like My Friends

Just because I hang around Larry doesn't mean I'll act like him. Sure, he drinks from time to time, but he never gets drunk. Besides, he's promised never to drink around me.

Mom says I do too much for my friends. She says they use me. But I really don't mind giving them rides. In all honesty, they probably wouldn't invite me if I didn't.

Making friends isn't as easy as it was when you were a child. Friends are now more than the people who invite you to birthday parties. They're the people who love you as you are and who encourage you to be the best you can be. They're the people who give advice for problems and encourage you when you're going through hard times.

Solid friendships require both giving and receiving. All friendships involve a series of choices:

Will you be true to each other? Will you say what you really think, believe, and feel, or will you say what your friend wants to hear? Will you encourage each other to live out Christian values or make each other hesitate?

Check God's Word

First Corinthians 15:33 explains that the people we spend time with always influence us, either for good or for bad. Obviously the best solution is to choose friends who live right and who motivate you to do the good you want to do.

Second Corinthians 6:14-16 encourages close relationships with those who live their faith in Jesus Christ. Remove the "not" from this passage and rewrite it positively to make it even clearer. After you've tried it yourself, read this sample:

> *Choose close friends who believe and live out their faith. Otherwise your differences will eventually divide you and cause conflicts. You'll try to obey God while your friend ignores God or tries to hide what he does from God. Choose friends who see the world the way God does. Then you and your friend will be able to create closeness that will make both you and God truly happy.*

Talk It Over with God

Talk with God about your friends:
- God, a friend who makes me proud to be a Christian . . .

- God, a friend who makes me hesitate to express my faith . . .
- God, my parents want me to have friends who . . .
- I want friends who . . .
- God, I'm discovering that pleasing You in my friendships also pleases me and pleases my parents. I see this in . . .

Apply It to You
God wants you to have the most sincere, fun, and caring friends around. In light of this, what changes do you think God wants you to make in your friendships? Realizing that no one is perfect, but no one should have too many excuses, how do you think God wants you to respond to your current friends? How do you think He wants them to respond to you?

3
They Don't Like My Dates

Just because his hair is a little long, my parents think he's on drugs or something.

She's shy, not snobby. Why can't my parents understand?

My dad always tries to match me up with somebody weird. Why won't he let me pick my own dates?

Parents react strongly to the people you date for three basic reasons:

Hope. They want you to find happiness with someone for a lifetime. When they see negative personality characteristics in your date, they fear you'll lose your chance for happiness.

Fear. The AIDS epidemic and high teen pregnancy rate make parents afraid for you to date anyone. They don't want you to have sex and then pay for it the rest of your life.

Timing. If you're dating one person seriously

when you're still in junior high or high school, you risk neglecting other important relationships. A broad spectrum of friendships now is great preparation for happy romance later.

Which of these three factors (hope, fear, timing) seems strongest in your parents?

Check God's Word

Proverbs 1:8, 9 suggests that parents have wisdom worth listening to. Of course, no parent is right all the time, but most of what parents say has some truth to it. The more your parents listen to God, the more sense their advice makes.

Because people didn't "date" in Bible times, there are no direct references to dating in Scripture. But there are hundreds of verses about love and closeness. Think about what dates would create the type of relationship happiness described in these verses: Hebrews 10:24; Ephesians 4:31, 32; I Thessalonians 4:3, 6a, 9b; Matthew 6:33, 34a.

Talk It Over with God

Talk with God about dating: your view, your parents' view, God's view.

- God, I think my mom/dad is wrong about the person I like when . . . but right when . . .
- God, what do You think about the person I like? What do You want for my romances?
- Realizing that You created male/female attraction and You want me happy, I want to fit into Your plan. Help me understand . . .

Apply It to You

Respond to your parents' *hope* by considering their comments. Ask: "What do you hope for my dating life?" "What kind of person do you think would make me happy?"

Relieve your parents' *fear* by establishing firm sexual limits and then assuring your parent of your decision to wait until marriage for sex. Invite God to empower you to do what you say you'll do.

Establish your own best *timing* by recognizing that pairing too early can short-circuit your relationship skill development. Make it a point to keep friendships strong and to ration your dating time.

4

They Make Me Do Too Much

A: "What do they think I am? A slave? I hate to clean toilets. Why am I the one stuck with the bathrooms?"

B: "I have to wash dishes every night, and I really get tired of it."

C: "It's my room and I ought to be able to keep it the way I want it."

Betcha thought these were all teen quotes, didn't you? Actually, Mom says "A" when she has bathroom duty. And when Dad washes dishes and would rather have his feet up reading a good book, he says "B." And both parents said "C" after their son dropped his soccer gear in a living room chair after they'd spent all afternoon getting the house ready for company.

Of course, their teenager has said all the same lines at various times, too. Face it. Nobody likes housework.

Check God's Word

Ephesians 4:16 suggests that the best solution involves everyone doing some of the work and enjoying some of the pleasures. The verse describes the church as a body, and Christian families are a part of this body.

Ways to build up family members in the midst of chore conflict include:

- Compliments: "You did a good job on the yard today."
- Appreciation: "Thanks for helping me clean up for Nancy's visit."
- Cooperation: "Can we work together on this to make it go faster?"
- Humor: "Let's list all the things we hate about cleaning bathrooms!"

Ephesians 5:21 reminds us of another important ingredient in successful relationships. Submission means to place another's needs before your own. It has also been defined as voluntary yielding in love. When everyone in the family submits, no one will feel taken advantage of or used. Each will look for ways to do his or her part of the yuck work, and each will recognize chores as ways to care for the other family members.

Sound like an ideal? Of course. But it's an ideal worth working toward.

Talk It Over with God

Use these sentence starters to talk with God about work at home:

- God, it doesn't seem fair when . . .
- Realizing that we all have to do some of the yuck work, I wouldn't mind doing . . .

• Submitting to my family becomes easier when I realize I'm doing it for Jesus . . .

Apply It to You
Work with your family to divide up chores evenly and according to skill. List all the things that need doing, the approximate time it takes to do each, and how often they need to be done. Then divide them among yourselves.

Alternate: What can you do if your family doesn't want to divide things equally? How does God want you to respond if you really do more than your share? if another member of your family is overburdened?

5
Movie and Music Wars

My parents always bug me about what I watch and listen to. I agree that some stuff in movies and on TV goes against God's plan. It's not right to go to bed with someone you're not married to. It's not right to use people to get what you want. It's not right to kill people with weapons or words. But there's not much else on. And just because I watch it doesn't mean I'll do it. I know what I believe, and I'll obey God.

Face it. There aren't many good shows to see or hear. So you've got to pick and choose carefully. The cure for the movie and music blues is to do your own evaluating. You can choose shows, songs, and movies that encourage you to live what you believe, rather than those you have to get over, ignore, or make excuses for. We all need help to grow romances, friendships, and confidence. Choose media that help you do so.

Check God's Word
The media issue is a complex one. Read these Scriptures and add your thoughts to the ones printed here.

- Philippians 4:8
  Many people excuse destructive words in songs by saying they like the music best. But music helps the words stick in your head (that's why commercials use music). How important do you think it is to choose songs with words that encourage God's way of life?
- Proverbs 23:7a
  How heavily do you think thoughts affect actions? How much effect does what you read, watch, and listen to have on your lifestyle and decisions?
- Matthew 12:34b, 35
  How important are the beliefs and life-style of the characters in a show or the artists who play the music?
- Luke 9:50
  How important is it that the actor or artist be a Christian if the message is true and agrees with the Bible?

Talk It Over with God
Talk with God about movies and music.

- God, my parents and I disagree about movies, music and other media when . . . but we agree when . . .
- God, how do movies, TV shows, and songs influence me?

- God, the true values in the last movie I saw
were . . . The twisted ones were . . .

Apply It to You
Why do you think music, television, and movies
bring about such conflict between parents and
teenagers? What actions would bring
understanding?

You have an advantage over your parents'
generation because Christian music, videos, and
books are now available in great variety. Look for a
Christian band that plays the style of music you
most enjoy. Then you can have the music you like
with words that encourage you to find happiness in
ways that work—God's ways.

Fairness

1

My Brother Gets Away with Everything

When my stepmom's son does something wrong, she gives him a lecture. When I do something wrong, she grounds me or calls my mom. Then I face double trouble.

When I was my sister's age, I didn't get to go to as many places or stay out as late as she does. All she has to do is whine a little and Dad lets her go all the places I now go. It's not fair.

Check God's Word

Some unfair situations are simply pesky. Others are genuinely unfair. Many are created by circumstances beyond your control. When you go through family problems created by your parents, by you, or by tough situations, claim the promise found in II Corinthians 4:8.

Fill in the blanks with your situation: "I am hard pressed by . . . , but not crushed; I am perplexed by . . . , but not in despair; I am persecuted by . . . , but not abandoned; . . . strikes me down, but God will not allow me to be destroyed."

No matter how unfair things get, God can teach

you through the bad, or turn that bad into something good. Lean on Him.

Talk It Over with God

Talk with God about what He wants you to do about your unfair situations. Rather than simply endure, try actions that unite and equalize.

Caution: Life is never totally fair. Work toward balance, but don't expect perfection.

- I'm upset because I want my parents to . . .
- When I think my parents are being unfair, they're probably being . . .
- Sometimes my parents really are unfair. How do You want me to respond?
- God, thanks for protecting me from ultimate harm when I go through rough times like . . .

Apply It to You

Prepare a "talking guide" containing specific words and actions that could increase the probability of understanding and being understood in unfair situations. Examples:

THIS	INSTEAD OF THIS
I know you don't mean to, but . . .	You did that on purpose.
I feel as though you favor my brother.	You never consider my side.

Now use these words and actions. Refuse to let your parents or siblings dictate how you will respond. No matter what they say or how they say it, respond with the attitude and words of Christ.

69

2

They Won't Let Me Have What I Want

My parents won't let me buy or even ride a
motorcycle. They think I'll hurt or kill myself.
What really gets me is that my dad had a
motorcycle when he was a kid. He says
they're more powerful and dangerous now. I
think he just doesn't remember how good
riding a motorcycle feels.

Obedience is tough when you're certain you are
right. This is the time to let honor step in. The most
effective obedience grows out of honor. How would
you define "honor"? (Let Webster's help if you like.)

Did you include images such as "value,"
"consider the ideas of," "admire," "respect," "give
credit to," "cooperate with," "accept," "give
attention to"? Or did you limit your definition to
"bowing as though to royalty"?

Notice that honor is not blind obedience as
much as it is caring about your parents enough to
understand and appreciate their guidelines.

When you understand your parents' reasons, you'll find it easier to obey.

Check God's Word
As your honor leads to obedience, notice in Ephesians 6:1-3 that honor brings a promise.

Ask your parents to help you understand the reasons for their rules and the good they are trying to achieve. For example, perhaps your parents want to give you literal "long life on the earth" by forbidding the motorcycle. In that case, brainstorm with them about other ways you might obtain and enjoy the "motorcycle feeling."

Ephesians 6:4 explains that obedience is a two-way street. It's easier to honor and obey parents who don't irritate you and who help you understand how and why they want you to do what they ask. How can you ask for this?

Ideally, obeying your parents' guidance brings you up in "the training of the Lord." The more you and your parents listen to God, the more joy you'll all receive.

Talk It Over with God
Remembering that all parents are exasperating sometimes and all children fail to honor sometimes, talk with God about obedience.
- God, my parents exasperate me when . . .
- I fail to honor them when . . .
- I could make it easier to honor and obey my parents by . . .
- I could make it less likely for my parents to exasperate me by . . .

71

Apply It to You

Write a series of hints for dealing with disagreements. Choose hints that will work in your family. For example, when discussing disagreements, always point out an area of agreement first: "I think you're right that motorcycles are dangerous, but I would always wear a helmet.'"

Ponder your last disagreement with your parents. Mentally relive it in a way that would show honor. How does honor ultimately bring about the results you want? the results your parents want? the results God wants?

3

"If I Were a Parent, I'd . . ."

When I get to be a parent, I'm going to trust my teenagers. I'll lighten up and not worry so much.

I won't be so strict. I'll give my teenagers freedom.

I'll listen more and lecture less.

Why do parents do all the things teenagers hate? Sometimes because those things need to be done. Other times because parents let their own worries, shortcomings, and uncertainties creep into parenting. Your parents struggle with issues similar to the ones you struggle with: liking themselves, feeling confident about the decisions they make, trusting God to take care of worries, getting other people to like them. You just might change the way your parents act by giving them some of the understanding you crave.

Check God's Word

When you feel frustrated and angry with your parents, you may want to blast their weaknesses. Before you do, read Luke 18:9-14, especially verses 9 and 14.

Feeling angry with and oppressed by your parents is okay. Letting those feelings continue or develop into contempt is not. To keep from being overly critical of your parents, think about your own weaknesses. Then talk calmly about your feelings.

When you're angry about the way your parents parent, back off and look at the circumstances. Notice elements that are beyond your parents' control. Recognize pain they may be experiencing. Search for elements in their background that might make it hard for them to love you the way they want to love you. Then observe any contribution you may be making to the problem.

Notice ways you and your parents fuss and fight rather than swallow pride and work together to solve problems. Pray for your parents and for yourself. Work with them to move from failure to success, from inflicting pain to understanding, from self-sufficiency to admitting needs.

Talk It Over with God

Talk with God about the things you wish your parents would and wouldn't do.

- God, it seems so obvious that my parents should . . .
- God, because we're a family and families are made to work together to solve problems, help us to . . .

- When I'm a parent, help me remember . . .
- Right now, help me to . . .

Apply It to You
Put on your parents' shoes for a moment. How would you handle these situations?
- Your teen won't talk about what she does and thinks. You want to be close.
- Your teen stays out past curfew.
- Your teen chooses a friend who seems to drag him down rather than bring him up.
- You suspect your teen is using drugs.
- You're so proud of your teen that you don't know how to say so.

Which of your parents' parenting patterns do you want to repeat? Which do you want to change—and how would you change them?

If you're really brave, write yourself a letter of advice on how to raise teenagers and put it someplace safe. Read it after the birth of your first child!

4

My Parents Don't Get Along

My parents keep saying they love each other.
I wish they'd show it.

If my folks would accept each other's quirks
instead of fighting, they'd get along.
Nobody's perfect.

Whether your parents fight, are separated, or have
divorced, you can draw on God's power for dealing
with the pain of parental discord.

Check God's Word
God wants families to express love rather than
inflict pain on each other. So why does He let
family pain happen? So he can give us freedom.
Unless we choose to love, it's not love at all. Sadly,
the same freedom that allows true love allows
opportunity to inflict pain.

Most parents don't mean to hurt each other or
their children; they are just continuing a
destructive pattern they've learned. You can seldom

MY PARENTS DON'T GET ALONG

change the way your parents act, but you can decide two things.

- You can choose to reject divisive patterns in your own relationships. Read Deuteronomy 30:19b, 20.

God can help you create happiness both now and in your future if you choose to let Him. Because you've experienced your parents' patterns, your natural tendency will be to repeat them. But you can use God's supernatural power to replace destructive patterns with actions that bring love.

- You can choose to look for and enjoy God's good plan. Read Jeremiah 29:11. God will not allow crises to foil His plan for giving you joy and security.

How might God turn your present family pain into hope? How might depending on Him bring you comfort during a family crisis? How might God work your present family pain into His good plan?

Talk It Over with God
Use these sentence starters to guide your talk with God about your parents' discord.

- God, I get so scared when my parents . . .
- God, I know that I can't blame myself for my parents' poor choices, nor can I mediate between my parents. Help me find the balance by . . .
- God, please motivate my parents to get along, particularly in the area of . . .
- The next step You seem to be asking me to take is . . .

Apply It to You
You can't change the ways your parents relate to each other, but you can choose whether or not you'll imitate them. Down the left column of a piece of paper, write word for word the last conflict your parents had. Now down the right column rewrite it as you wish it had gone.

Yelling, complaining, and accusing can mean there's a totally different problem lurking somewhere. What personal pain or past bad experience might be lurking behind your parents' lack of harmony?

5

They Always Put Me Down

How many times do I have to tell you to study harder? With grades like that you'll never make anything of yourself!

You look ridiculous!

How could you do such a thing to your parents?

Put-downs hurt like crazy, especially when they come from parents. Put-downs stay in our heads and convince us that we can't do or be anything worthwhile.

Possibly the worst characteristic of put-downs is that we tend to imitate them. Put-downs keep you from growing close to people, from being genuine. They keep you protected but lonely.

Check God's Word
Exodus 34:6b, 7 contains both a promise and a principle that apply to put-downs.

God promises to forgive and help us stop doing wrong. He wants to heal us and make us happy. But at the same time He realizes the persistence of sin: the effects of sin continue generation after generation.

Rather than repeating your parents' put-down patterns, choose to replace put-downs with uniting words. Do this by imitating God—He is compassionate, gracious, slow to anger, loving, and faithful. Only He can break the sin cycle.

Talk It Over with God
Talk with God about the way your parents talk to you:

- God, it hurts so much when my mom/dad says . . .
- God, help me to resist repeating the put-down pattern. I could start by . . .
- Some actions I could use instead of put-downs are compliments, encouragement, understanding, listening, . . .

Apply It to You
Invite God's help to break the put-down (or other sin) pattern.

- Step A: Don't believe the put-downs. Even when you fail, you are not stupid, worthless, or embarrassing. Rather than dwell on your mistakes, learn from them.
- Step B: Remind yourself that God made you, and He doesn't make mistakes or junk.
- Step C: Take definite steps to increase your confidence and self-esteem. Deliberately reteach

yourself that you have worth. A team of teenagers offers these tips:

> *Accept compliments.*
>
> *Talk out your frustrations with someone who believes in you.*
>
> *Share your successes with someone who will show pride in you.*
>
> *Worry about what's worth worrying about.*
>
> *Invite God's help to get your faults in perspective and to lessen them.*
>
> *Understand yourself.*
>
> *Stand up for your beliefs.*

• Step D: Consider cultivating a friendship with another adult for the support and encouragement your parents can't or won't give. Choose someone who offers genuine Christlike support.

Independence

1
I Want My Freedom!

Why do my parents have to hang on so tightly? Can't they see I have to make my own choices, even if some of those choices are wrong? Why can't they let go?

Jesus had three short years to prepare twelve disciples to take the good news of salvation to the entire world. How do you suppose He felt about granting independence to these disciples?

Your parents have had a few more years to prepare you to find your place in the world. How do you suppose they feel about granting you independence?

As your parents grant you independence, they have both great confidence and tremendous fear.

- They wonder if they've prepared you well enough, so they keep asking the same questions.
- They worry that you'll make the wrong choices, so they continue to tell you what to do.
- They want you to discover for yourself how obeying God makes a difference in everyday life, so they tell you what to believe and why.

- They want you happy, so they spend time explaining how rather than listening to ways you've already discovered.

   Working toward independence is almost as hard for parents as for teens!

Check God's Word

Jesus demonstrated that the secret to granting independence is good preparation and placing His loved ones in God's hands. Read the prayer Jesus prayed for his disciples before his death in John 17:6-26. Underline phrases your parents might say about you, putting yourself in the disciples' place.

Talk It Over with God

Talk with God about these verses and about your growing independence.

- God, Jesus' prayer shows me that Jesus wanted . . . for His disciples.
- What Jesus wanted is like what my parents want for me because . . .
- God, my parents have given me a foundation for independence by . . . I still need them to . . .
- My parents and I can continue to be close as I gain independence. We'll show this by . . .

Apply It to You

What actions, attitudes, or words indicate that your parents are having trouble giving you independence? How might you work together to make the process easier for both of you?

2

God Has No Grandchildren

What difference will God make in my life?

Have I made God mad by the bad things I've done?

I go to church—what else does God want?

One of the most exciting—and most difficult— aspects of independence is the opportunity to decide for yourself how close you will grow to God.

God has no grandkids: your relationship with Him cannot be determined by what your parents believe or don't believe. You decide whether or not you will become a Christian. You decide whether to depend on Him or to choose less-reliable sources of security (like money and status). Only you can get to know God and personally enjoy Him.

Check God's Word

The first faith step is to decide if you want Jesus to guide your life. This is called "accepting Jesus as

Savior and Lord" or "becoming a Christian."
Everything you do and think hinges on this
decision.

Read the following verses: John 3:16, 19, 21;
14:6.

- John 3:16 reveals that eternal life, life with both
  quality and quantity, comes to those who accept
  Jesus.
- John 3:19, 21 explains that Christians choose
  actions they're proud for others to know about.
- John 14:6 further explains that Jesus is the
  source of understanding, real life, and
  happiness.

Have you taken this first step of accepting Jesus
as Savior and Lord? If not, do so now by talking
with Jesus. Admit the things you've done wrong or
failed to do right. Ask Him to forgive you. Invite
Him to guide your future actions and thoughts.
Then begin the adventure of obeying and enjoying
God.

Talk It Over with God
Talk with God about your decision to become a
Christian, whether you made it today or in the past.

- God, I'm glad you've come into my life
  because . . . OR I want you to come into my life
  because . . .
- God, believing in You changes the way I view
  my future because . . .
- God, becoming a Christian is just the
  beginning. It's a process of knowing You and
  living for You. I think the next step for me
  is . . .

Apply It to You
How would (or how has) your becoming a Christian and obeying Jesus help(ed) your parents trust you more and give you more independence?

Think about adults you know who live out their Christianity. Choose one of them and ask that person questions like: "What have you learned that you wish you had known earlier?" "What is hard about living a Christian life and why is it worth it?" "Why are you glad to be a Christian?" "What is your favorite Bible verse and why?"

3
Am I Bad If I Doubt?

Is God really there?

When something bad happens, I wonder if it means God is mad at me. My mom says people do most bad things, not God, and that God is as sad as I am when those things happen. I wish I knew if she was right.

How do I know God answers prayer when I can't hear Him?

Finding answers to doubts and tough questions is a perplexing aspect of making your own faith choices. Many people believe it's bad to question God, that it shows a lack of faith. But in most cases, asking God about your questions and doubts shows more faith, not less. Just as you ask for homework help from the smartest kid in your class, asking God questions shows that you trust Him to have the answers.

Check God's Word

A disciple called Thomas once asked Jesus for proof of His identity. Rather than scolding Thomas for asking, Jesus gave him the evidence he needed. Read John 20:24-28.

Because God is real, plenty of evidence for Him exists. Develop the habit of taking your questions and doubts directly to God and letting Him give you answers. God wants you to trust Him enough ask, to listen, and to learn until you understand.

Talk It Over with God

Talk with God about a question, confusion, or doubt you have.

- God, I'm glad You don't mind my questions. I'm even more glad You have the answers. This makes me feel . . .
- One answer I already understand is . . .
- God, my doubts are strongest when . . .
- There are some things I may never fully understand this side of heaven, but I'd like a couple hints. One is . . .
- God, I know You are there because . . .

Apply It to You

Why do you think some people are afraid to ask God questions?

In addition to talking with God, talk with another Christian about your questions and doubts. Be cautious of pat answers or answers that make you feel worse instead of better. You might also ask for an article or book that addresses your question or doubt.

4

Earning My Keep

My parents say I spend too much. I say they don't know how much things really cost. They say I should be more concerned for quality than name brand. I say I don't want to be embarrassed at school by wearing out-of-style clothes.

What's the solution? Discover the value of money by handling some of your own and by asking God's guidance as you spend it. You'll gain another badge of independence: money management.

Use your allowance and extra earnings for spending money and entertainment. As your earnings grow, you can pay for more of your own needs and learn how to manage your own money. No matter what you earn, give ten percent off the top to church.

If your family situation requires that you use your earnings to meet family needs, realize that what benefits the family ultimately benefits you.

View your family as a team and make plays that will help the team win.

Budgeting family earnings takes cooperation and personal sacrifice which is seldom easy. If you get to feeling oppressed, remember that you have spent much of the money your parents have earned over the years. And remember that God has promised to meet all your needs (Philippians 4:19).

Check God's Word

As you earn and spend money, cultivate a view of money that matches God's view. For example, God wants you to depend on Him, not on money, for security. He wants you to see money as a way to buy things, not a way to buy happiness.

Find more insight into God's view of money in I Timothy 6:6-10. Underline the three phrases you think God most wants you to remember from these verses. Summarize these in your own words to help you remember and live God's view of money.

Talk It Over with God

Keep your Bible open to I Timothy 6:6-10 as you talk with God about the verses.

- God, being secure with You affects the way I view my money because . . .
- God, I want to be content with food and clothing, but I find myself unhappy unless I have certain kinds of food and clothing—especially when . . .
- God, some of the evils and griefs that come from seeking after wealth are . . .

- Because there are more important things than money . . .
- God, knowing You are interested in how I earn and spend my money . . .

Apply It to You
If your current earnings don't yield enough to buy your clothes, ask your parents to let you manage your clothing budget. This allows you to decide which items are important enough to sacrifice other items for. You can gain valuable experience in managing when there's no money left and in making the money stretch further next time.

5
A Clean Break

I need my parents, but I want them to see me
as self-sufficient. I want their advice, but I
want to make my own decisions. I want to
lean on them, but I still need respect. I have
outgrown some of the ways I need their love,
but now I need it in other ways. Can I have it
both ways?

Yes. The happiest independence maintains a
relationship with parents. This closeness is quite
different from the one you had as a child, but it can
be more meaningful. It is created by talking with
and relating to each other on a more mature level.
It grows as both you and your parents grow in God.

Check God's Word
The best family members draw their strength from
God and then share that strength with each other in
times of sorrow and times of joy. Compare your family
with the picture described in II Corinthians 1:3-5, 7.

The truly independent recognize their need for other people. What do you need from your parents: support? encouragement? listening? motivation? ideas? unconditional acceptance? What do they need from you?

Talk It Over with God
Talk with God about using your freedom to continue to love and relate to your family.
- Independent closeness includes being there for and listening to each other's important experiences. My parents and I do this by . . .
- God, because I don't need my parents' help for everything, I'm free to ask for . . .
- A comfort I can share with my mom or dad is . . .
- A sorrow I need to share with my mom or dad is . . .
- My parents and I can ease each other's suffering by . . .

Apply It to You
One of the best ways to express a more mature relationship with your parents is the way you talk with them. Choose exercises like the following to give God's "comfort" and "compassion" to your parents.
- Because you can't take harsh words back once they're spoken, translate before you speak. For example, translate anger into request: "Quit treating me like a baby!" becomes "Please listen or offer options rather than lecture." Or translate accusation into explanation: "You have

no respect for my feelings!" becomes "When you tease me in public it embarrasses me."

- Read I Corinthians 13:4-8 for attitudes and actions of mature love. Intentionally express these actions and attitudes as you talk with your parents.
- Rehearse it first. When you need to talk about something major such as asking for a new freedom, rehearse what you want to say and how you want to say it. Anticipate possible reactions from your parents and rehearse a response to each.
- Say thanks. Your parents are preparing you for interdependence. Let them know you appreciate the good job they're doing.